An Introduction to Special Educational Needs in Early Years

Edited by Tessa Knott

A NASEN Publication

Published by NASEN.
NASEN is a registered charity. Charity No. 1007023.
NASEN is a company limited by guarantee, registered in England and Wales.
Company No. 2674379.

Further copies of this book and details of NASEN's many other publications may be obtained from the NASEN Bookshop at its registered office:
NASEN House, 4/5 Amber Business Village, Amber Close, Amington, Tamworth, Staffs. B77 4RP.
Tel: 01827 311500 Fax: 01827 313005 Email: welcome@nasen.org.uk
Website: www.nasen.org.uk

Cover design by Raphael Creative Design.
Typeset by J. C. Typesetting.
Typeset in Times and printed in the United Kingdom by Stowes (Stoke-on-Trent).

AN INTRODUCTION TO
SPECIAL EDUCATIONAL NEEDS IN EARLY YEARS

Contents

An Introduction to
Special Educational Needs in Early Years

In the foreword to the *Curriculum Guidance for the Foundation Stage* (QCA, 2000), Margaret Hodge describes the early years as 'critical in children's development. Children develop rapidly during this time – physically, intellectually, emotionally and socially. The foundation stage is about developing key learning skills such as listening, speaking, concentration, persistence and learning to work together and cooperate with other children.'

The aim of this publication is to demonstrate how good practice in early years education can help all children, and particularly those with special educational needs (SEN), develop these key skills.

The book brings together a series of articles written by experts in the field of special educational needs, first published in *Early Years Educator* (2000/01) published by Mark Allen Publishing Ltd. It represents an easily accessible introduction to some of the range of special educational needs that can be met in early years settings and suggests practical guidance and strategies.

Two strands that run consistently throughout the book are the need for early identification and the critical importance of working with parents and carers.

Teachers in England and Wales will know that the Special Educational Needs and Disability Act (2001) and related Codes of Practice for Schools make an increasing assumption that children with special educational needs will be educated in mainstream settings.

Jo Armistead's helpful opening piece guides the reader through the legal expectations and provides reassurance about the agencies and professionals who are there to support. She also offers practical tips on how to help when a child gives cause for concern, based on careful observation and record keeping to identify where the child is having problems.

The SEN Code recognises that not all children develop at the same rate, but stresses the need for 'carefully differentiated learning opportunities to help them progress and regular careful monitoring of their progress'. It also encourages early years settings to communicate effectively with parents, drawing on their knowledge and understanding of their child and raising any concerns they may have about their child's needs and the provision made for them. These strands are emphasised throughout the book as key to good practice.

Throughout the book early years educators will find the expert advice they need to welcome all children and their parents into their setting.

CHAPTER 1:
Children with special educational needs in early years settings: How confident do we feel?

Jo Armistead

Children with identified special educational needs (SEN) form a small minority in early years settings. Due to the low incidence many of us feel inexperienced in and unprepared for the responsibilities of teaching a child with a significant disability. Parents of children with medical conditions that are diagnosed in infancy will initially express their feelings of inadequacy and a sense of pain and loss for the child that they might have had. Teachers and nursery or playgroup staff feel a similar sense of not being up to the challenge, and not being in control, when first asked to meet the needs of a child with significant developmental delay or with a disability. They talk of loss of sleep, of loss of confidence and feelings of anxiety. However, the SEN agenda and parental expectations are changing the pattern of provision for children with special needs towards the inclusion of all children into early years settings, and early years staff are developing their skills accordingly.

What are our responsibilities?
Early years practitioners in maintained nurseries and reception classes and in registered early education settings for three and four year-olds have the same responsibilities for the identification of and provision for children with special educational needs. The requirements of the Special Educational Needs Code of Practice apply to them. These include the need to have an SEN policy and a staff member responsible for the co-ordination of special educational needs in every setting. The Foundation Stage refers to the diverse needs of children. It states that for practitioners an awareness and understanding of disability and of the Code of Practice is essential. It recommends:

- the use of a wide range of teaching strategies;

- the provision of a wide range of opportunities to motivate, support and develop children and help them to be involved, concentrate and learn effectively;

- the monitoring of children's progress to identify any areas of concern and taking action to provide support by using different approaches, additional adult help or other agencies.

These responsibilities apply to all funded three and four year-olds.

What are special educational needs?
Children have special educational needs if they have a *learning difficulty* which calls for *special educational provision* to be made for them.

Children have a *learning difficulty* if they:

a) have a significantly greater difficulty in learning than the majority of children of the same age;

b) have a disability which prevents or hinders them from making use of educational facilities of a kind generally provided for children of the same age in schools within the area of the local education authority;

c) are under the compulsory school age and fall within the definition at (a) or (b) above or would so do if special educational provision was not made for the child.

Children must not be regarded as having a learning difficulty solely because the language or form of language of their home is different from the language in which they will be taught.

Special educational provision means:

a) for children of two or over, educational provision which is additional to, or otherwise different from, the educational provision made generally for children of their age in maintained schools by the local education authority (LEA), other than special schools, in the area;

b) for children under two, educational provision of any kind.

(from *The SEN Code of Practice,* DfES, 2001)

From September 2002, the Special Educational Needs (SEN) and Disability Act (2001) will apply to all schools and early educational settings. The duties under the Act make it unlawful to discriminate, without justification, against disabled pupils in all aspects of school life. There is a requirement that all schools will draw up accessibility plans to:

* improve access to the curriculum;

* make physical improvements to increase access to education and associated services;

* make improvements in the provision of information in a range of formats for disabled pupils and parents.

Children with a disability
The definition of children with learning difficulties includes children with a disability where any special educational provision needs to be made. This does not mean that children with a disability necessarily have learning difficulties, nor that only disabled children with learning difficulties have special educational needs. It means that all children with a disability have SEN if they have any difficulty in accessing education and if they need any special educational provision to be made for them, that is, anything that is *additional to* or *different from* what is normally available in schools in the area.

Disabled pupils and prospective pupils are covered by the duties in the Special Educational Needs and Disability Act. A disabled person is defined as someone who has a physical or mental impairment which has an effect on his or her ability to carry out normal day-to-day activities. The effect must be:

* substantial (more than minor or trivial);

* long-term (i.e. lasted or is likely to last for at least a year or for the rest of the person's life);

* adverse.

Discrimination is either:

* treating a disabled pupil or prospective pupil less favourably for a reason relating to his or her disability than someone to whom the reason does not apply without justification; or

- failing to make reasonable adjustments to admission arrangements and in relation to education and associated services to ensure that disabled pupils or prospective pupils are not placed at a substantial disadvantage in comparison with their non-disabled peers without justification.

The duty not to treat a disabled pupil less favourably and the duty to make reasonable adjustments are the two core duties that lie at the heart of the disability discrimination provisions in education.

What are the responsibilities of the local authority?

Local education authorities have a responsibility to support all settings to meet their responsibilities to children with SEN. Through their Early Years Development and Childcare Plan, they will have made arrangements for training setting special educational needs coordinators (SENCOs), using part of their early years standards fund allocation and other specific grants. They have a responsibility to set up a network of area SENCOs, in the ratio of at least one area SENCO to 20 early years settings.

They must also make support services available to children in any early years setting, and provide advice to staff. These will include learning and pre-school support, sensory support, Portage and educational psychology services.

How are children with SEN identified?

By their third birthday, most children will have had two statutory health checks to assess their development. This means that a small number of children turn up at their pre-school setting with an identified medical condition or syndrome, or they may have a sensory impairment affecting their sight or vision. About 2% of the child population will have a significant developmental pattern that will have an effect on their pace or style of learning and that will require additional teaching support. The amount of extra help will vary according to the individual child.

Even by three, depending on their developmental need, this group of children will be known to health professionals, including speech and language therapists, physiotherapists and occupational therapists. Nowadays, it is also likely that they will be known to a specialist pre-school teacher, a teacher for children with visual or hearing impairment, or a Portage worker, who will have got to know the child at home or in a play setting. A few children will also be known to an educational psychologist. These people will be able to offer advice and support when the child moves on to take up a place in nursery or playgroup. Admission forms should include space for parents to provide information about their child's additional needs and any other service supporting the child.

A small number of children will have a Statement of Special Educational Need, which will specify a level of support or resources that the child must receive, as well as the priorities for learning. This may involve the support of a non-teaching assistant or a specialist teacher, and the attention of a health professional, or the Statement may require physical adaptations to furniture or a building, or a specialist teaching programme.

In many areas, children with the most severe developmental delay will attend special schools, but parents and local authorities are beginning to look to these children being included in mainstream settings. There are longstanding examples of profoundly disabled children attending community pre-schools to the benefit of both the child and their family.

Among the school population there is another group of children, an estimated 18%, who will have a range of additional learning needs that should be identified by their teachers and carers, and whose needs should be met within their setting, be it school or pre-school. Within the early years, the proportion of children with learning needs is not likely to be so high. However, within any group of young children there will be some whose development causes concern to their teachers and carers and their parents.

What are the most common developmental needs in the early years?
Staff working in early years settings will be aware that a number of children will have some degree of immature or delayed development. The most commonly referred difficulty is speech and language delay. Immature production of speech sounds and unclear speech or lack of speech, and language difficulties, for example poor understanding, are the most common forms of delay. It has been estimated that one in five children under seven has some form of delay in these areas. It is probably underestimated how difficulties in this area can be linked to behaviour – with children being frustrated when communicating their needs or just not understanding what is going on.

Other difficulties which cause concern and which early years staff often identify are more general, but may indicate a developmental learning difficulty or disorder. These problems can involve children having problems concentrating, being easily distracted, or having physical problems and coordination difficulties. They may fall over, or bump into things, or avoid large play equipment or fine motor tasks. Other difficulties can involve social or emotional difficulties, being socially anxious or over-boisterous.

If you suspect that a child has a problem, how do you help?
Always start by making observations of the child to get some idea of the extent and the nature of their special educational needs, to find out in what area of development the child has a difficulty. Think about what you as an adult can do to help the child and note what approach is successful. Keep a record of the progress the child makes. If the child continues to cause concern, arrange to talk to the parents, and to the health visitor for a pre-school child, to discuss referral to other agencies. In a school setting, you should also discuss the child's needs with parents and refer the child to the SENCO.

Always involve parents in any decisions you make for their child, including planning a teaching programme or making a referral to another support service. Meet regularly with parents to celebrate the successes and to continue to plan for the future.

The effects of Government policy on SEN are gradually being seen in all early years settings, as practitioners become more confident in their abilities to provide for all children. Additional resources of the personal kind are being developed and early years workers are discovering an understanding of the range of child development of which they were previously unaware.

Strategies to be used by practitioners in early years settings

- Plan a programme of short activities to develop skills and maintain concentration.

- Use signs or pictures or say key words to help a child's understanding of situations.

- Modify tasks by breaking them down into smaller stages.

- Start some complicated tasks from the end rather than the beginning, e.g. ask a child to replace the final piece from a puzzle rather than replacing all the pieces to start with.

- Reduce the choice for children who might find too much choice confusing, e.g. painting with two colours or playing with a small number of construction pieces.

- Offer open-ended activities so the child can learn the process rather than produce an imposed outcome.

- Model big play and small play by playing alongside.

- Use verbal and visual prompts to help children who need repetition and practice before they can master concepts.

- Ensure that children know what is going to happen during the session – using photographs can help.

- Use praise and appropriate rewards – reducing rewards as children gain in competence.

- Offer firm but reassuring boundaries.

- Talk children through physical tasks to provide a verbal prompt of the sequence of actions involved.

- Be positive and share the child's success with them and their parents – show the child how they are making progress.

- Match a child with a more competent friend for a short period of peer supported learning.

AND

- Make sure your provision is imaginative and rich in offering a wide range of sensory experiences to help children develop all their senses.

- Provide access to messy play, and physical play outside, so that children have the opportunity to manipulate dough, clay, earth and sand to develop fine motor skills and to move freely in large spaces to develop gross motor skills.

- Recognise that these experiences have a calming, therapeutic effect on children too!

Getting organised and working with others

- Develop your special needs policy and review it annually.

- As the area SENCO network is developed, use it to share experiences with neighbouring settings and build your confidence together.

- Tell parents how you provide for children with special needs in your welcome brochure.

- Get to know your local health visitors and speech and language therapists.

- Share information about nursery activities with a child's speech therapist, who can reinforce concepts and vocabulary.

- Work closely with other therapists to plan children's activities in your setting.

- Look out for special needs training provided by your Early Years Partnership.

- Find out about the pre-school services or Portage service in your area, and call them in to offer support and advice.

- Check out your local toy library for specialist toys for children with special educational needs.

CHAPTER 2

Key to early intervention

Dr John Visser

How can we give children with SEN the best start in life?
There is now little doubt that the quality of the physical and emotional experiences in our early years lays the foundation for our later achievements. It is as well to remember that this view of early years has not always been the prevailing one, particularly in the area of special education needs.

Previous generations have viewed disability as being governed by inherent defects, 'bad blood', a time when the 'sins of the fathers' were visited on the children, and even that your facial features were the key to predicting your handicap. We now understand the biological and environmental aspects of child development much better and have come to a greater understanding of the interactional dimensions of nature and nurture.

Understanding this interaction plays a key part in meeting young children's needs as they grow and develop into adolescents and adults. This understanding is of particular importance to those young children with special educational needs. The interaction of biological and environmental factors may place some children at particular risk of developmental difficulties.

Early intervention can contribute significantly to the progress these children make and at a minimum can mitigate the negative impact of these difficulties. An important development arising from the increased professional understanding of the interaction of nature and nurture has been greater awareness of involving parents in interventions.

Previously, there was a focus upon assessing and intervening solely with the child, leaving parents to one side and overlooking the importance of their contribution in the identification and assessment of their child's SEN. An emerging further development is the involvement of the child, seeking, where possible, his or her participation in this process and his or her views on the form of intervention, particularly where this involves placement in a specialist setting.

More widely, there is a growing recognition that families with children with SEN should be regarded holistically, having their needs met by links between the service providers. This holistic approach needs to be underpinned by agreed principles.

Key principles
The key principles outlined below are common to all ages and stages in life. However, they are of particular importance in the early years because of their ability to have long-term positive effects. Young children with SEN do not grow out of them. Without intervention by parents, professionals and provision, their SEN will lead to reduced educational achievements, with all that follows. These principles provide the framework for interventions that will enable children in their early years to maximise their potential. NASEN has identified eight key principles. NASEN's Policy document on Early Years, sets out key principles which could help providers develop their own SEN policies and include:

• **Early intervention:** the importance of the identification and assessment of SEN at the earliest possible stage cannot be overstated. This should be done in a close working partnership between the parents/carers and relevant professionals.

- **Priority of access:** no society has limitless resources. Children with SEN and their parents/carers need to be accorded priority in accessing appropriate support and provision. Without this access, they are unlikely to achieve their potential, socially, emotionally, physically or academically. Investing in early support and provision will enable many, if not most, young children to gain these achievements and unlock their potential to become independent, successful adults alongside their peers.

- **Equal opportunities:** young children should not be prevented from accessing the same range of educational and social opportunities as are available to their peers. Some children may need specialist provision which takes them away from their peer group for a time, but this should only be the case where it is in the best interest of the child. The greatest amount of inclusion should always be the paramount objective in meeting the needs of pupils with SEN. If we wish to have a tolerant, inclusive society, then from the early years there is a need to ensure that 'exclusive' practices are eliminated.

- **Individual needs:** in this respect the provision, support and help provided should be tailored to meet the individual strengths and needs of children. These differ from child to child, even within the same area of disability. This requires flexibility on the part of services and professionals, particularly in how they respond to individual differences.

- **Parental involvement:** parents/carers have a wealth of knowledge and understanding of their child which needs to be drawn upon in all aspects of assessment, provision and intervention. A partnership between parents/carers and professionals which is based upon confidence, trust, transparency and openness is required if children in their early years are to have their needs met.

- **Provision:** it is important that children with SEN have access to a range of provision which can be matched to their age, abilities and needs. Provision needs to match the child rather than the reverse, given individual differences in needs. Without a range of provision, there will be a tendency to make the child fit the provision to the detriment of meeting the full range of his or her needs. Wherever possible, provision should be within the local neighbourhood setting. Where children with SEN are placed within mainstream settings, the quality of this inclusion should be high. High quality inclusion means that the child is a full and equal member of his or her peer group, and is a full and equal member of his or her class.

- **Training and support:** both parents/carers and professionals can enhance their understanding of children's SEN with training and support from more experienced practitioners. Knowledge and understanding of SEN helps to provide insight when identifying, assessing and most importantly providing. The skills required to meet the range of children's SEN do not come naturally, they come with experience and training.

- **Shared responsibility:** running through some of the above principles as a constant theme is the need for an integrated, coordinated and consistent approach to meeting the individual child's needs. This requires close working relationships between professionals and with parents/carers. It also means that agencies should work together strategically to ensure that appropriate policy, provision and practice is in place to meet the full range of child and family needs.

These principles are important but need implementation if they are not to become dry aspirations sitting upon policy makers' and providers' desks. Much has been put in place to facilitate professional practice based upon these principles.

For example, there is a requirement that LEAs establish early years development and childcare partnerships. This development has the potential for closer working partnerships in meeting the needs of young children with SEN. The current Government has education high on its agenda, and within that it has been reviewing all aspects of special education.

The programme for action for SEN places great emphasis on early intervention, by which they mean, not only early identification and assessment, but also early action to meet young children's SEN. Early excellence centres and Sure Start projects are to be welcomed, not least because they focus on the importance of early years and bring new resources to it. But these initiatives and others are often unclear about their role with the child with SEN, who frequently receives little or no mention in the guidance documents which accompany them.

There remains a need to ensure that these initiatives and ongoing practices and provision are linked so that there can be continuity and coherence in meeting children's needs. Parents need to see some consistency of approach over time. Partnerships take time to develop; often these initiatives are short-term and can 'wither on the vine' once new funding initiatives and budget shifts occur.

To prevent a drift back to the 'bad' old days when children with disabilities and SEN were labelled, categorised and frequently marginalised; where the causation of these difficulties was placed upon superstition, class or a particular physical feature; a degree of vigilance is required. Organisations such as NASEN play a key role in ensuring that the needs of children with SEN are kept to the forefront in educational debates.

It is to be hoped that as science attempts to identify the exact function of each human gene, society and educators do not lose sight of the effects of nurture on the development of children, nor the effects of the principles outlined above upon the creation of a society and education system that provides the very best nurturing for young children with SEN.

CHAPTER 3:
The vital link between home and school

Helen Emad

A good working relationship between parents of children with special needs and professionals in education is a must

It has long been recognised that the involvement of parents throughout their children's education reaps benefits for all concerned. However, when a child has been identified as having special educational needs, it is even more important that parents have access to information and support to enable them to play a valued and active role in the intervention planned for their child.

Partnership with parents is a theme that runs like a thread throughout the DfES Special Educational Needs Code of Practice (2001). Under the revised Code of Practice, the Government will require all LEAs to make arrangements for parent partnership services, the aim of which is to ensure that parents have access to information and support so that they can make appropriate, informed decisions in relation to their child's education.

In 1994, LEAs across England and Wales were invited by the DfEE to submit bids for funding to set up parent partnership schemes. Most LEAs set up parent partnership schemes within their existing SEN services, others commissioned the work to a local voluntary organisation, usually one with an established record of expertise and credibility in the area of children with disabilities.

At that stage, parent partnership schemes were largely envisaged as a means of facilitating parental involvement in the statutory assessment of children with SEN. Much of the focus was on improving parents' access to information, and on supporting them in contributing their written views towards their child's statutory assessment. They also sometimes needed help in understanding often complex and bewildering procedures involved in the formal assessment process and the range of options available to children in relation to educational placement and types of provision.

Parental rights

Following the implementation of the 1993 Education Act, a SEN tribunal was set up, under the auspices of the Secretary of State for Education and Employment, giving parents stronger rights of independent appeal against decisions made by their LEA in relation to their child's needs. Since then the numbers of parents using the SEN tribunal has steadily risen. The positive side of this is that it shows that parents are becoming more aware of their right to have a say in important decisions about their child's education, partly as a result of information provided through parent partnership services.

However, the SEN tribunal is proving to be an extremely expensive way of resolving disagreements between parents and LEAs, the full cost of which is met by Government funding. It is not only in financial terms that the price is high; the process of appeal can often be lengthy and stressful for all concerned and relationships between parents and professionals can sometimes be damaged beyond repair.

In an attempt to address these issues, the revised Code of Practice requires LEAs to strengthen arrangements for providing conciliation in early stages of dispute. Frank discussions throughout the assessment process can only serve to improve communication and cooperation between professionals and parents and help to avoid the kind of misunderstandings that are often at the root of major disputes about SEN provision.

Listening to parents

Parents need to feel that they are being listened to and that their opinions matter to the professionals. The revised Code of Practice highlights the benefits to parents of having access to support and advice that is completely independent of the LEA. Parent partnership services have vital links with independent parent support networks. Even where parent partnership schemes have not had their base within a voluntary agency, it is recognised that the voluntary sector as a whole has a unique contribution to make in supporting parents of children with a range of special needs.

There is not only an expectation that LEAs will work closely and consult with voluntary agencies in their area, but also that schools and other providers of education will actively seek out information about local voluntary and parent groups and make sure that families are aware of these other avenues of support.

An important shift in the revised Code of Practice is to offer partnership services to all parents of children with SEN, not just those who have a Statement or who are undergoing statutory assessment. This acknowledges that many parents and carers need access to support and information from the point at which their child's special needs are first identified.

Early identification of SEN

The DfEE *Programme of Action for Meeting Special Educational Needs* (1998), which was the forerunner to the revised Code of Practice (2001), stressed 'the importance of early identification and appropriate intervention to improve the prospects of children with special educational needs and to reduce the need for more expensive intervention later on'.

Only a small minority of children with SEN have difficulties that are evident in the first year or so of life. Apart from those children with the more severe learning, physical or sensory disabilities, it is notoriously difficult to reliably identify the nature and degree of a SEN in the pre-school years.

Often, it is the parent who first raises concerns about his or her baby or toddler's development. This may be after many months of niggling anxiety. The manner in which professionals approached with such concerns respond can be critical in laying the foundations for future work with the child and the family.

All parents are different in their values, perceptions, aspirations and personalities. Getting to know the parents of all the children in the early education setting is the first step towards a positive working relationship.

Making parents welcome

To ensure that parents can be in partnership, it is important that no unnecessary barriers are preventing or inhibiting communication between the education provider and parents. Parents need to feel that they are welcome in the nursery and that staff have the time to discuss issues in confidence.

Some parents have unhappy memories of their own school days or may lack confidence in communication skills. Others may not have English as their first language. These factors can often make parents reluctant to approach staff to discuss concerns about their child.

If a parent fails to attend meetings or reviews about the child, or does not appear willing to participate in therapy programmes, this does not necessarily indicate that he or she is not interested. Sometimes, parents are overwhelmed by their child's difficulties and find them too distressing to talk about.

For other parents, their child's SEN may be relatively insignificant compared to other difficulties they are experiencing in family life, such as poverty, illness, depression, housing problems or unemployment.

Transparency in SEN policy

Early education providers have a duty to provide written information to parents describing their policy on meeting children's SEN at all stages. For most children, extra support will be provided from the resources and skills already available within the setting. Sometimes, parents will have to be informed that their child does not meet the criteria for resources or services that they believe their child needs. Openness and transparency in discussions with parents is crucial to a relationship of mutual trust.

Encouraging parents to engage in the programmes of intervention planned for their child will often help them to feel more positive and instil in them the confidence that they too can play a vital role in the child's progress alongside professional input.

A multi-agency concern

The basic principles underpinning partnership with parents of children with SEN are the same principles as should apply to all parents. However, where additional needs are identified, partnership with these parents in planning and involving them in appropriate interventions is fundamental to positive outcomes for these children throughout their career in education. If parents feel from the outset that they are supported, informed and respected as equal partners in decision-making, some of the extra pressure of caring for a child with SEN will be eased.

Partnership with parents has a high profile throughout the revised Code of Practice. The effectiveness of this will depend on a genuine commitment on the part of all providers of education, statutory and voluntary agencies to work in close collaboration and cooperation with one another and with parents, carers and children and young people with special needs.

Parent partnership services, wherever they are based, will continue to promote the good practice already evident in many early education settings, and also to ensure that parents know where they can access appropriate and relevant information and support as and when they need it.

CHAPTER 4:
Learning to seek clarification

Maggie Johnson

How active listening can and should be promoted in early years classrooms, and how to go about doing it

Children with speech and language impairments are frequently unable, unwilling or unaware of the need to seek clarification when they do not understand spoken language. Many are passive in their interactions with adults, tending to wait for direction, reminders and explanations rather than ask for them.

When faced with linguistic overload, many employ a range of conversational fillers or distraction techniques rather than acknowledge that they do not know the answer or cannot follow the discussion. They frequently attempt to answer questions or carry out instructions without true understanding, apparently operating on the basis that if they give their best attempt, someone more knowledgeable will stop or redirect them if necessary.

Other children who are less likely to seek clarification include those who are under-confident, have low self-esteem or lack conversational experience – a significant proportion of many mainstream reception classes.

Functional vs verbal

Consider the two exchanges that follow:

Adult: Could you fetch my wallet, please?
Child A: Here it is.
Adult: Could you fetch my wallet, please?
Child B: What's that?
Adult: It's got my money in it.
Child B: Here it is.

Both children have understood what was required of them; they both demonstrate good functional comprehension. Child A may have a more extensive vocabulary and score higher on tests of verbal comprehension, but in practice it does not matter because child B was able to seek clarification.

Observation of children with normal language development indicates that the ability to compensate for poor understanding develops as a natural part of language acquisition. As soon as a young child shrugs or says 'What?', they are either implying or verbalising their need for clarification.

Seeking clarification or 'active listening' is an important skill to cultivate, as ultimately it enables children to cope with the increasing demands of their educational and community settings. As all teachers will be aware, it is often hard to retrieve the loss of self-esteem experienced by children who feel helpless in dealing with their problems, confusion and failure.

This perhaps is the strongest argument for ensuring that active listening skills develop in the early years, for having access to a repertoire of appropriate and effective clarification strategies is fundamental in gaining a sense of control over one's environment and social interactions.

Ironically, what is generally seen as good classroom practice often results in removing the need to seek clarification and the opportunity to practise these skills.

Focused support may actually encourage children to rely on adults to 'bail them out' rather than develop their own compensatory strategies. The answer, however, is not to remove that support, but to consider alternative ways of providing it.

What active listening involves

Active listening is something we practise when someone has not succeeded in getting their message across. It may occur in noisy pubs, in a foreign country and during rushed or careless conversations. The table (on next page) summarises the main reasons for conversational breakdown with examples of appropriate clarification strategies. Active listening involves:

- attending to the speaker;

- taking responsibility for understanding the message;

- being aware that messages cannot always be understood;

- acknowledging non-comprehension;

- active participation in repairing any breakdown in communication.

Active listening is particularly important for children with comprehension difficulties and short attention spans as it allows them to:

- check they have understood instructions correctly (this includes compensating for the use of non-literal language);

- check they have heard someone correctly;

- cope with an unfamiliar accent or dialect;

- gain time while they write something down or work something out;

- compensate for when they switch off;

- cope with different teaching styles.

Intervention programme

Staff at Gap House School have developed an active listening programme based on the work of Dollaghan and Kaston (1986). It can be introduced at any age, but is particularly relevant in the early years when good habits formed will benefit children throughout their education.

A whole-school approach is recommended, with full parental involvement for any children experiencing particular language or learning difficulties. There are two strands to intervention: whole-class approach (creating the right environment) and group work (targeting specific active listening skills).

Creating the right environment

The following suggestions can be adopted by all adults at home and school on an opportunistic basis throughout the day.

- Promote the message that it is good to ask, and praise any attempt to imitate or initiate clarification strategies. Be careful to commend the high-achievers when they seek clarification, so that others need not associate asking for help as a sign of failure.

- Indicate one's own need for clarification rather than guess when children omit information, for example, 'Can you tell me a bit more – I don't know who you're talking about.' 'I'm confused – you didn't say when this happened.'

- Explain to children that they will not always know what adults are talking about, but it is alright as long as they let the adult know. Refrain from giving clarification as soon as a child gets stuck. Make it clear that help is available, however, with phrases such as 'I could say it again if you like', 'Is there a word you did not understand?', 'Show me the bit that's difficult.'

- Acknowledge children's confusion or errors by modelling appropriate clarification strategies, for example, 'I don't think you've heard of a raccoon before, have you? If I say a word you don't know, you can say 'What's that?' 'If you can't remember all of it, just ask me to say it again.' 'That's a good try, but it's not quite right. Why don't you ask me which one I need?'

Please note that it is important to use natural dialogue as the vehicle for developing active listening rather than the information aspect of curriculum delivery. The main objective of the latter is to provide the child with clear, unambiguous facts and explanations which the child can understand easily.

Group work

Group sessions of mixed ability provide the opportunity for children to learn from the interactions between the facilitator and others in the group. The size of the group will vary, depending on resources and organisational constraints; many mainstream schools use trained learning support assistants to facilitate small groups, while others have incorporated the ideas into a whole-class topic, circle time or school assembly. Therapists and teachers may choose to lead the groups in language units and specialist nurseries, either jointly or alone.

Reason for breakdown	Example	Seeking clarification
Impossible content	Child is asked to do something but a necessary item is missing, e.g. 'Cut these out, please.'	Where are the scissors?
Rate	Speaker talks too quickly.	Slow down, please
Volume	Speaker talks too quietly.	Pardon?
Competing noise	Background noise.	I can't hear you
Inexplicit/Ambiguous	Speaker omits vital information, e.g. 'Put it over there' or 'Pass the red one.'	Which one? Where does it go?
Contradictory	Speaker makes a mistake and changes name in mid-instruction, e.g. 'John, read the next page. Come on, Tom.'	Me or John?
Unfamiliar vocabulary	Vocabulary is outside the listener's experience.	Is tugging like pulling?
Too long	Child has poor verbal memory	I can't remember all that
Complex grammar	Child has comprehension difficulties, e.g. 'Before you go out to play, finish your work.' (It is simpler to say, 'Finish your work, then go out to play.')	What do you mean?

In the pre-school years

Teach what is meant by 'listen!' by breaking it down into three behaviours:

- Sit in your own space (without distracting others).

- Look at the speaker.

- Think about the words (talk about the same thing as the speaker).

Label each behaviour using pictures, signing and symbols as appropriate. Practise each behaviour individually before expecting children to combine them. Develop awareness that it is not always possible to understand:

- Introduce notion of 'silly' or 'alien' words in contrast to 'real' or 'sensible' words. Associate these words with human and non-human characters.

- Present simple instructions or questions using these words, giving praise for saying 'I can't' or 'I don't know' or laughing at the strange language. Intersperse with legitimate requests.

- Introduce more subtle contrasts (for example, knife/life or brush/comb) inviting children to stop you when you have said the right word.

- Give instructions using these off-target words, asking children to hold back until you have said the right word.

- Ask children to decide if requests or statements are sensible or silly, using the 'impossible' category of conversational breakdown initially. Work from a hidden picture so that children can see the intended meaning after each example ('Walk on the ceiling!' for example).

Once children have developed these foundation skills, the concepts of 'knowing', 'guessing', 'working it out' and 'understanding' will be far easier to grasp at Key Stage 1. Children will be more receptive to adult models of phrases such as 'I don't know' and 'What do you mean?' and benefit from the opportunity to seek clarification in activities designed for interaction and problem solving.

Most importantly, they will appreciate what is meant by 'Tell me if you don't understand' and 'Ask if you need help' – stock teaching phrases which all too frequently fall on deaf ears.

- Grateful thanks are extended to Catherine Martin, Elizabeth Roberts and Paul Catherall, for taking the lead in introducing and developing active listening approaches in the UK. This article is an edited version of *Promoting Understanding of the Spoken Word Through Active Listening,* published in the proceedings of The Naplic Conference, 2000, University of Warwick.

Further reading

Dollaghan, C. A. and Kaston, N. (1986) 'A comprehension monitoring program for language-impaired children', *Journal of Speech and Hearing Disorders*, Vol. 5, pp.264–271.

Johnson, M. (1991, 1996) *Functional Language in the Classroom – a handbook for parents and professionals.* Manchester Metropolitan University, Clinical Communication Materials.

Key points

- Stock teaching phrases such as 'Tell me if you don't understand' or 'Ask if you need help' frequently fall on deaf ears.

- Seeking clarification or 'active listening' is an important skill to cultivate, as ultimately it enables children to cope with the increasing linguistic demands of their educational and community settings.

- Over-dependence on learning support assistants frequently removes all need for language and learning impaired children to seek clarification.

- The answer, however, is not to remove additional support, but to consider alternative ways of providing it.

- Children are helped to recognise non-comprehension, seek clarification and improve their functional comprehension.

- Having access to a repertoire of appropriate and effective clarification strategies is fundamental in gaining a sense of control over one's environment and social interactions.

Useful materials

'Good Listening' and 'Good Talking' classroom posters. Available from Taskmaster Ltd. Telephone: 0116 270 4286.

CHAPTER 5:
Communicate if you want to educate

AFASIC

How can you help young children with communication problems reach their full potential?
The ability to use spoken language is a skill many of us take for granted. But for thousands of children, it is not that simple. And because language is a vital medium for learning, a delay or disorder in the capacity to use or understand speech can have a profound effect on a child's development.

These children have a speech and language impairment that is primary or specific (not, for example, the result of deafness or physical disability), though because language is so fundamental it is likely to affect other areas, such as literacy or behaviour. For some, however, a specific language difficulty may coexist with other conditions, such as moderate learning difficulties or cerebral palsy.

Estimates of the numbers of children with speech and language impairments vary considerably, depending on the level of severity at which children are included. The concept of a spectrum of difficulty, from mild to severe, is useful here; counting only children with complex, long-term impairments will yield a very different result from including every child with a difficulty, however transient.

Recent studies suggest that at least 7% of pre-school children have some degree of language delay or difficulty which could affect their ability to learn. Local initiatives in some parts of the country, however, indicate that this figure could be higher, maybe as many as 35%. Of these children, about one in 500 has severe difficulties which persist into adult life.

Definition
Speech and language impairments vary in cause and in nature, as well as in degree. For most children with speech and language impairment, their difficulty is developmental. Some children, however, acquire speech and language impairment through brain injury or as a consequence of some specific forms of epilepsy. It is also worth remembering that a history of glue ear, and the accompanying intermittent hearing loss, can contribute to difficulties in spoken language development.

A major distinction is between comprehension (understanding language) and expression (using language). Most children with an impairment will be more able in one area than the other, though many have difficulties in both and the two are to some degree interrelated. A child with a speech and language impairment may have difficulties with any or all of the following:

- Articulation: the mouth, tongue, nose and breathing mechanisms, and how they are coordinated and operated by muscles.

- Phonology: the sounds that make up language.

- Syntax or grammar: the way words and parts of words combine into phrases and sentences.

- Semantics: the meaning of words, parts of words, phrases and sentences.

- Pragmatics: how we use language in different situations, and convey feelings.

- Intonation and stress (prosody): the rhythm and 'music' of the way we speak.

- Memory: the ability to retain information in the short or long term.

General problems with movement (dyspraxia), attention or sequencing can profoundly affect the ability to acquire language. Some children with difficulties in the area of semantics or pragmatics will be included within the 'autistic spectrum'. A considerable number of children whose problem is regarded as behavioural will in fact have a speech and language impairment that has not been identified.

Symptoms and behaviour

Difficulties with articulation or phonology are more obvious, and more likely to be recognised early than more complex problems of semantics or pragmatics. Some subtle disorders are only identified much later, as curricular demands on children's communication abilities become greater.

Children with comprehension difficulties may be labelled 'naughty', not doing what they are told, behaving aggressively or being overly familiar. But the excessively quiet child may also have a problem: is she just shy? Or does she not really understand what is going on? Some children, for psychological or emotional reasons, choose not to speak at all in certain situations: this is known as 'selective mutism'.

A variety of identification and assessment tools are available for use in the early years. The use of WILSTAAR, developed by speech and language therapist Sally Ward, is spreading, often as part of Sure Start schemes. Ann Locke's Teaching Talking is also useful, and the benefit of both approaches is that they include practical ways of working with children once their needs have been identified.

For many children with speech and language impairments, self-confidence and self-esteem are major issues. Children who find it difficult to communicate are likely to find themselves increasingly isolated from their peer group. They will need help and support to make friends, overcome their isolation and boost their confidence.

Finally, of course, language is a vital prerequisite for the development of literacy. AFASIC and the British Dyslexia Association, together with Glaxo Wellcome, are examining in more detail the links between language difficulties and later difficulties, and developing training packages for professionals.

What can be done to help?

A wide range of conversational opportunities is essential for communication. For children with speech and language impairments, there is a danger that as they become increasingly isolated due to their difficulties opportunities for conversation reduce further, accentuating the spiral of isolation. Communication, like charity, begins at home, so working with parents is vital. The Hanen programme, developed in Canada but increasingly used in the UK, enables professionals to equip parents with the skills to develop their child's language in the home.

Do communicate with parents about the reasons for carrying out particular exercises or activities. For example, explain that the reason for working so hard on joint attention is that attention is a fundamental part of communication.

It may sound obvious, but children need experiences to talk about. The wider the opportunities (indoors and outdoors, sights, sounds and smells, animals, objects, music and visits), the more substance there will be to conversation and the greater the extension of language use. This is one of many reasons why play is so important in the early years.

Children also need to be exposed to a wide vocabulary, moving beyond concrete nouns to verbs, adjectives, adverbs and abstract nouns. They need to hear language in use, in one-to-one conversation or group story time. It is, however, possible to overload and nursery professionals need to be sensitive to the pace of language development with which individual children can cope.

Phonic games are a familiar but important way of reinforcing language, while music and rhythm activities develop children's awareness of pattern and skills in auditory discrimination. Other skills underpinning language use, such as memory and attention, can also be practised through appropriate games and activities.

Finally, the local speech and language therapy service has particular expertise in child language development. Effective information sharing and joint working between professionals of different disciplines is essential if children with difficulties are to receive the help they need. Therapists operate an 'open referral' system: any concerned parent can make an appointment directly.

Key skills
- Attention: make sure the children look at you when you speak. Practise good sitting and concentration.

- Sequencing: games and activities involving sequences and 'putting things in order'.

- Memory: games and activities ('I went to the shops and I bought...', Kim's game).

- Phonology: verbal games with rhyme and alliteration ('I spy', nursery rhymes).

Hints and tips
- Speak slowly and clearly.

- Simplify your speech.

- Give instructions in the order in which they are to be carried out.

- Repeat key words and information.

- Expand simple utterances (e.g. Child: 'Teddy chair'; Adult: 'Yes, teddy is sitting on a chair').

- Model correct use (e.g. Child: 'Teddy falled over'; Adult: 'Yes, teddy fell over, didn't he?').

CHAPTER 6:
The long and winding road to literacy

Dorothy Smith

For some children, acquiring reading skills is a bit of a struggle

To become a fluent reader, one requires a knowledge of both visual and phonological tasks in order to provide meaning from words and books. Readers recognise letters and words as visual patterns, and from memory, need to put a spoken label onto them. Readers understand how the language is composed of a variety of sounds which can be written in many different ways. They are able to manipulate these sounds orally and use this knowledge with unknown written words.

They also have good language skills, both receptive and expressive, so that they can gain understanding and meaning from what they read. Thus reading is a complex skill which most children master over the course of their time at school. Children do not learn to read at the same rates. Some children learn to read before they enter school or even before they go into nurseries. They find the whole process easy.

However, most children develop reading skills far more slowly. Reading is dependent upon their language skills, their visual processing abilities and their phonological awareness and competence. Teachers and nursery nurses need to be able to observe and informally assess reading 'behaviours' and skills.

Assessing reading skills

Some of the following questions may need to be answered by parents but when they are all answered they will build up a profile of the young child as a reader or one who may find reading difficult.

The child's feelings about books

- Does the child enjoy being read to?

- Does the child listen quietly when read to and for how long can he or she sustain concentration?

- Does the child choose to look at books both at home and in the book corner?

- Does the child ask for books as presents?

The child's interactions with the text

- Does the child pretend to read when looking at a book? (Does he or she make up a story as if he or she is reading?)

- Does the child read the pictures?

- Does the child show interest in the stories by asking questions or making comments?

- Does the child answer questions that are asked by the adult about the story? (Does he or she imagine what might happen next, and can the child explain what might be happening?)

- Does the child show an ability for retelling common stories?

- Does the child join in when a well-known story is read or when a nursery rhyme is recited?

- Does the child supply a word for the end of a sentence?

The child's knowledge of print
- Does the child seem to understand that the black marks on the page can be read? Does he or she know that the adult is actually translating the squiggles on the page into words?

- Does the child understand that the marks on the page are separate words? (This is a skill that might not be understood in the pre-school or early years setting.)

- Does the child show that he or she can point to individual words? (As with the previous question, this is a skill that might be understood when words such as McDonalds or Lego are given, but not within a sentence or a piece of text.)

- Does the child show that he or she can see the difference in the shape or length of words?

- Does the child show that he or she can match similar words?

The child's phonological awareness
- Does the child recite nursery rhymes or jingles independently?

- Does the child indicate that he or she understands that some words rhyme (sound the same)?

- Does the child supply a rhyming word for a given stimulus word?

- Does the child play 'I spy', thus indicating an awareness of the initial sounds within words?

- Does the child show an ability to give the initial sound of a spoken word?

Within nursery classes, any work undertaken with reading can be indirect and often child-led. Reception classes are required to work within the literacy hour where the framework is more prescriptive. However, teachers in reception classes will still need to differentiate their teaching for those children who are found to have few early reading skills.

Books and stories
When choosing books for use in early years settings, it is important that these:

- are enjoyable to both the reader and the children and can be reread without interest being lost (children love humorous stories);

- are not too long and can be joined in with ease;

- sound interesting when read out loud;

- have a predictable and powerful story line (sometimes containing stories already known to the children);

- have a distinctive layout and contain good illustrations which complement the story;

- are repetitive (often stories containing rhyme or rhythm are successful).

Picture books are also important resources. The adult needs to be aware of those children who have not had early book experiences, as these children need to be read to individually, be drawn into answering questions, be encouraged to retell and pretend read and be invited to turn the pages when the story is being read.

Knowledge of print

There are many word matching activities where children can start to see the differences in length and shapes that can be devised. Common logographs can be recognised. The labelling of familiar foods in packets and tins can be discussed, as can shop names and TV titles. The child's own name is an excellent starting point, as often this will be different from all the others in the class.

The adult, by pointing to individual words, will model to the child that a particular block of print is being reproduced in speech, especially if the word is repeated (e.g. 'Run, run, run,' said the cat). No instructional teaching of word recognition is being given here. The early skills of visual processing are being built up before the child is ready to learn both letter names and sight words.

Phonological awareness

To build up children's awareness and skills in the aural and oral side of the language of words, there are many activities which can be given both directly and incidentally. Children need to 'hear' and discriminate between similar words so even if the words 'same' and 'different' are difficult, the children can respond with 'yes' and 'no'.

At first, words should be concrete and when different, be very different, such as 'cat' and 'umbrella', until later words like 'mouse' and 'house' can be supplied which are dissimilar in only one phoneme. Repeating and learning jingles and nursery rhymes are the forerunners to understanding about rhyming words.

Silly words that rhyme from children's names can be made up and at odd times in the day, children can be given the chance to 'play with words' until they are capable of supplying any word that rhymes with another. Many books for children are full of strong rhyme and rhythm. Before 'I spy' is played, children need to be able to hear and produce the sounds at the beginning of words, until later they are fully aware of this activity well before they have to connect the sound with a written symbol.

To conclude

Children do not acquire the skills of reading at the same time. Some will have continuing problems throughout their school-lives. Others will be slower to learn than their peers. The teaching of reading cannot be rushed. It needs to follow the pace of the child. If staff in nursery and reception classes identify the children who lack early reading experience and build up this experience, then these children will have the beginnings of those foundations necessary for later skills teaching. The love of books has to be engendered from as early an age as possible.

CHAPTER 7:
Why it is not as easy as 1, 2, 3

Olwen el Naggar

Early years professionals can help young children with difficulties in numeracy get better at maths

Some children enter school with an established profile of learning needs, for example, those with physical difficulties or profound and multiple learning difficulties. But if a child arrives at school unable to count, does this child also have special educational needs? Billy is one of these children. Although he has acquired some counting skills, there are many gaps in his learning. 'One, two, three, four, seven, I can count,' says Billy.

Billy appears to be able to count to four, but if four objects are placed in front of him, he is just as likely to say there are two objects as seven. So what is happening here? Billy's unaccomplished counting skills could be due to a variety of different reasons. Perhaps he has had little opportunity to develop early counting skills and would benefit from an enriched curriculum that offers him a variety of opportunities at the very early stages of counting. Measured against national targets for his age group, he is likely to catch up.

Perhaps Billy will progress at a slower pace than other children and experience difficulty with remembering and recalling previous knowledge, or with assimilating new knowledge and will always need a wide variety of experiences at each stage of development. Measured against national targets for his age group, he is unlikely to catch up. Billy could have a specific learning difficulty and may need alternative strategies at particular points in his development. Measured against national targets for his age group, he could meet, exceed or fall short of these targets at any stage in his schooling.

The mathematics to be taught to each of these groups of children would be the same, but the teaching style would need to change to match the learning needs of the children within the different groups. Whatever his special learning need, to be able to count successfully, Billy will eventually need to be able to carry out six processes. They are:

- Match: Billy will need to be able to understand what he is being asked to count and know which items are to be included in the count.

- Sort: he will need to be able to sort all the items in the count from those that are not in the count.

- Order: he will need to be able to place the items to be counted in an easy order to be counted, e.g. a line.

- Recall: he will need to be able to recall all the number words in conventional sequence.

- Pair: he will need to be able to pair the number words to the objects in one-to-one correspondence.

- Name: he will need to be able to name the final number in the count and know that it is the number of the set of objects.

What Billy brings with him to each lesson (his strengths) is central to his learning programme, this is his starting point. How closely his strengths match the targets for his age group will dictate the amount of support he needs. The type and severity of learning differences will determine what kind of specialist support he may need.

For Billy to demonstrate all his strengths in counting, he should be assessed on all six counting processes. A full profile can then be compiled. A sound list of hierarchical skills in the form of teaching objectives will help his teacher to guide him through his programme, however irregular his learning patterns may be.

The skill of counting the number of bricks placed in front of him (however small the number) assumes that Billy understands what he is being asked to count (match), knows the number words in sequence (recall) and understands one-to-one correspondence (pair). He has not been given opportunities to show if he can sort and order, or name the number of objects in a given set, but let us consider the three items that he has been assessed on.

Matching

Sometimes the position of objects in relationship to each other, their size or colour can be confusing to a child and cause uncertainty as to what he or she is going to count. Instructions like, 'show me which bricks you are going to count' and questions like, 'are you going to count all the bricks?' enable the child to focus upon the items to be counted and lessen misunderstandings about the task.

Recalling

At this stage, Billy not only has to remember the number words and know that words like 'two', 'seven' and 'ten' are number words and that words such as 'sock', 'apple' and 'dog' are not, he also has to remember the number words in sequence. Only through repetition and practice will he sort out and learn the arbitrary order that makes up the sequence of number words.

There is nothing to understand at this stage, counting is just a string of number words that must be memorised. They must be memorised in a certain order called 'the counting order' and until they are committed to memory, children are unable to count. Many children enter school already able to count at least to ten. There are, however, a few children (and adults) who always find counting difficult because they have sequential memory problems.

Faulty sequencing ability affects recognition of number patterns at all levels and can be visual, auditory or both. For Billy at this stage, it is auditory as nothing has been written down. Children who are making little or no progress need to work within a limited range of numbers. If they are presented with too much at once, it can cause memory overload and total loss of focus on the task in hand.

We need to start all counting activities with them by counting to one number beyond the point at which they begin to experience difficulty. If we start with small numbers and build up gradually, the child will never be beyond the point of achievable success. This does not lead to underestimation of the child's ability as the programme progresses with the child.

Such a programme can always offer the child the opportunity to practise a number that is too easy, but, if possible, never make the challenge too difficult, as children need to have confidence in themselves to be successful. There are also some children (and adults) who, although they know the number words in sequence, because of poor oral motor skills, have difficulty counting.

These children need to move onto using 'digit cards' more rapidly than others. As oral counting is not one of their strengths, they can easily feel excluded from whole-class oral work. Alternative ways of including them must be explored. Their own specific learning difference may also need one-to-one attention.

Activities for counting

Rhythm sometimes helps children to remember the sequence of numbers and those suited to this level of development should be multi-sensory. Examples of multi-sensory activities are:

- kinaesthetic: stamping and clapping;

- auditory: counting the number of chimes of a clock or the beats of a drum;

- visual: counting the swings of a pendulum.

Although number rhymes and whole-class chanting can help children to memorise the counting sequence, the degree of success is governed by sequential memory differences, and progress can be slow.

Pairing

At this stage, Billy is required to count by pairing the number words with the object being counted, one number to one item. The current vogue to start counting from zero can cause problems. Technically, zero is not a counting word, the first counting word is one. If we do not have anything, we do not count it. This is very important for children who are at the one-to-one correspondence stage of number development.

When they match the number words to the objects being counted, they invariably get a false reading. The seeds for the visualisation of the cardinality of a set are being sown at this stage and visualising the wrong number of members in a set could impede progress.

If this happens, it is very difficult to 'unlearn'. Try getting the child to 'slap' the empty space before the first object as they say 'zero', which sometimes works. Coordinating a sequence of sounds with finger control is primarily a sensory-motor skill, not necessarily associated with quantities. Many children arriving at school have not mastered this skill.

Dyspraxic children have particular difficulty and find it easier to count large objects that have been widely spaced. They need matching activities with everyday items: children on chairs, coats on pegs. They also need a variety of multi-sensory activities. Gaining these important early skills in mathematics needs to remain fun. While working towards the educational targets set for children with special needs, it is important that we make the journey as enjoyable as the arrival at the destination.

CHAPTER 8:
How ICT can help with 'dys-abilities'

Judith Stansfield

How can information technology help young children with 'dys-abilities' reach their full potential?

Young children starting out on their education are usually excited and eager to learn from all the experiences made available to them. Some children may have some physical or sensory differences that can cause access difficulties and others may have one or more 'dys-ability' and would prefer to learn in a style different to that of their teacher.

The most frequently occurring dys-abilities* and their associated problem areas are dyslexia (reading and spelling), dyspraxia (poor coordination and handwriting), ADD/ADHD (attention and memory), dyscalculia (numeracy) and Asperger's syndrome (social interaction). As many as 20% of the population may have anything from a slight tendency to a severe problem with at least one or two of these dys-abilities*. The average classroom is likely to have at least one child with quite severe difficulties and one or two with lesser problems.

Learning styles

Everyone has a preferred learning style, be it visual, auditory, tactile or a combination of any of them. We are all different: my learning style is strongly visual/tactile and I have problems with auditory memory, which means I must write down phone numbers and shopping lists to remember them. In the learning process, all strategies will be used at different times, but any individual will prefer one over the others.

Difficulties occur where there is a large mismatch between the child's learning style and the teacher's teaching style or where a child has a weakness in one or more cognitive area which makes progress along the normal route difficult. Young children are rarely able to adapt the instruction to their preferred style. It is much more likely that they will give up and 'switch off', develop avoidance strategies (e.g. going to the toilet, sharpening pencils, forgetting to bring books) or become an attention seeker/behaviour problem.

Early diagnostic screening

Until quite recently, the parents of children with one or more specific learning difficulties had to wait until their child had really failed, before any intervention took place. The problems their child faced daily were deemed developmental and it was believed that the child would grow out of them. Some children did, but there were many whose specific learning difficulties were not identified early enough, because it was difficult to run psychological tests with very young children.

This is still the case, but it is now possible for teachers to screen very young children and obtain some insight into their preferred learning styles. Ideally all children should be screened, as:

• It is not always immediately obvious which ones may have potential dys-abilities*.

• It can pinpoint physical problems of poor or intermittent visual and auditory discrimination.

• It benefits all children if the teacher knows how to target the teaching.

Even if the children are not screened, there are certain indicators to look for. Many parents know from early on that their child is different, especially where there has been a family history of difficulty in acquiring literacy and/or numeracy skills.

This may appear in the child as extreme clumsiness, a disinclination to paint or draw, or a penchant for jumbling syllables/word order. Other indicators include a child who is still not speaking as fluently as the other children or is very forgetful of instructions.

How can ICT help?

Children with dys-abilities* need a multi-sensory environment with a wide range of activities and equipment to develop and practise their newly acquired cognitive skills. This is the usual provision in a nursery class and ICT has its place in providing an additional means of supporting learning by:

- providing a multi-sensory learning environment with sound, images and animation;

- facilitating the creation of individualised work files and activities for a child;

- bypassing some coordination obstacles, by providing other means of recording information;

- supporting home/school collaboration in the learning process, especially where the home has a good computer, so routine overlearning of skills can be done in other ways, daily and in regular short stints.

What sort of hardware?

Unless there are coordination problems, the child does not need specialist hardware, just access to a good multimedia computer, more regular access than would be the class norm and extra supported practice in areas of weakness. Alternative access devices, if needed, should be made available for the child (rollerball or touchscreen, for example).

A rollerball is a large trackerball, with a latched select button. Many young children find this easier to handle than a mouse, as two hands can be used, one to move the pointer on the screen and the other to select the chosen object. There are many attractive trackerballs, but avoid the ones where the ball lifts out: they may be used for other activities!

Even more immediate is the interaction through a touchscreen, where the child can tap on objects on the screen to make choices or move things around. Many young children find this easier to use and to understand than a mouse, especially for early cognitive work.

Big keys is an alternative large key keyboard, with only letters and numbers and a few basic functions. Some children find it less distracting than a full keyboard, when they first start writing. Stick-on lower case letters can be added. An overlay keyboard, with customised paper overlays, can be useful for matching, sorting and sequencing as well as for early writing activities.

What sort of software?

There is a wide selection of software available for developing cognitive skills in mainstream classes. Most of it is attractive, multi-sensory and enjoyed by all the children. For children who are just beginning to read, talking books enable them to 'read' before they can read all the words. This helps to support the idea that reading can be fun and that interesting things can be discovered. A talking word processor stimulates early attempts at writing, especially where there are supportive word/picture banks on-screen or on an overlay keyboard.

Below are some titles that have been found especially useful. They are suggestions and should not be seen as a definitive list.

CD-ROMs: *All my words* and *Clicker 4* (Crick Computing), *Blob* (Widgit), *Choices* (Widgit), *Claude and Maud* and *Speedy Keys* (Brilliant/Semerc), *Inclusive Writer* (Inclusive Technology/Widgit), *Intelli Keys* (Inclusive Technology/Semerc), *First Keys to Literacy* (Widgit), *Learn More about Maths, Learn More about Words* (Lara Mera), *Millie's Math House* (Edmark), *My World* (Inclusive Technology/Semerc/REM), *Spider and friends, Spider in the kitchen* and *Switch on games* (Inclusive Technology), *SumOne* (Resource), *Tizzy's Toybox* (Sherston).

Talking books: *Living Books* (Broderbund), *My first amazing dictionary* and *PB Bear* (Dorling Kindersley), *Naughty Stories* (Sherston).

It is always better to prevent, rather than have to cure, learning differences. Provision along these lines will help to lay a firm foundation for progress, for children whose dys-abilities* could otherwise cause problems in later schooling. Most of the suggested software and peripheral equipment cannot be bought from high street shops. It may be purchased direct from the publisher or one of these specialised agents:

AVP: Tel: 01291 625 439; Fax: 01291 629 671.

Don Johnston – Special Needs: Tel: 01925 241 642; Fax: 01925 241 745.

Inclusive Technology: Tel: 01457 819 790; Fax: 01457 819 799.

REM: Tel: 01458 253 636; Fax: 01458 254 701.

SEMERC/Granada Learning: Tel: 0161 827 2719; Fax: 0161 827 2966.

Key points
- Establish the preferred learning styles of all the children to facilitate more focussed learning and teaching.

- Provide a multisensory learning environment and make use of the variety of equipment in the early years classroom.

- Use the child's strengths to support any learning differences.

- Use the computer as and when appropriate.

- Foster close home/school links for good collaborative support.

---

* Throughout this article, the word 'dys-ability' has been used for young children with learning difficulties usually associated with dyslexia, to highlight the fact that these children are often 'able' but have learning 'differences' which will easily become learning 'difficulties' if they are not addressed.

CHAPTER 9:
This approach is a sound way to go

Hannah Mortimer

How music could help children with special needs in early years settings develop more harmoniously

This approach was developed in North Yorkshire in order to meet a practical problem. When registered early years providers became required to 'have regard to the Special Educational Needs Code of Practice', many were unsure as to what their duties were. How were they to set about identifying and monitoring the special needs of children in their settings and what might an 'inclusive' early years curriculum actually look like?

I wanted to develop a practical training approach which not only introduced the special needs procedures, but provided a practical way of combining early learning goals and individual educational plans for any children with special educational needs. Given that as many as one in five children might have SEN at some point in their educational career, this seemed to be a worthwhile goal.

The result is the 'Music Makers Approach' now published by NASEN and evaluated through a doctoral research project at Sheffield University.

Why music?

Music is an amazing thing. It stills a crying baby. It captures a toddler's attention. It holds the interest of children who, in any other situation, might be experiencing considerable learning or communication difficulties. It provides opportunities for even very young children to join together sociably in a group, long before they are old enough to attend an early years setting.

It encourages children who find it hard to move to move more freely. It encourages children who do not like to look and listen to do just that. And, above all, it is fun. As such a powerful tool, it is not surprising that music can be used very effectively to teach young children to learn and to develop.

In the Music Makers Approach, a regular music session is planned as part of the early learning activities for the whole group. Not only does this become a useful way of working towards the early learning goals for the foundation stage of learning, but it can be used to welcome and include children with a wide range of special needs.

Perhaps you have a large group of children who are still at the stage of settling into your early years setting. Perhaps they still find looking and listening difficult, especially when they are learning within a large group. Perhaps you feel it would be worthwhile planning approaches that help all the children develop their attention skills, learn how to cooperate in a group and develop the confidence to 'have a go'. Music making would be one way of approaching this.

You may have already identified some children within your group who have SEN. Perhaps you have a child who has physical or coordination difficulties, a child who finds it hard to concentrate and to learn, a child whose behaviour is challenging or a child who has difficulties in seeing, hearing or using language.

Perhaps you are keen to develop approaches that will include all the children fully in your curriculum, yet which are exactly targeted to meet the special needs of any individual child as well. The Music Makers Approach is an excellent tool for your tool box.

Getting started

Look for a regular half-hour slot each week when you will be able to have a 'Music Makers' session. Many settings choose a slot towards the beginning or end of a session so that any parents, and particularly those of children with special needs, can join and share the enjoyment. Once a group is up and running, you may be able to invite other parents of pre-school children with special needs in your locality to join for the half-hour session.

Find a quiet area where the children can sit down in a circle. An ideal area is the story mat of a playroom or classroom. The idea is to define the boundary clearly (a mat or a cushion shows the children exactly where to sit) and to have all the children and adults able to face both each other and the leader; hence the idea of the circle.

Young children and some of those who have SEN may well wish or need to sit next to a parent or adult, or on a parent's knee. You will need to start collecting musical instruments. Percussion instruments such as shakers, drums, bells, tambourines and wood blocks are most useful. You can usefully build this into a project on music or sound, helping the children to make a range of percussive and shaking instruments.

You will need musical accompaniment. Perhaps you can harness some local musical talent and encourage a neighbour, colleague or parent to play the piano for you, or raise funds for an electronic keyboard. If not, a cassette or CD player can work well.

Organising your session

In the Music Makers Approach, each session follows a set pattern; the sense of routine and familiarity becomes important to the children. First, choose a well-known and favourite song to signal the beginning of a session: this will become your 'theme tune'. This warm-up song lets the children know that music is about to begin, makes them feel secure with its familiarity and immediately gives them an action to do to get going.

You then need a greeting song to welcome all your children into music time. You should greet each child with a name, a look and a smile, perhaps a wave too. Ideally, you should encourage the children to look at you as you sing, and respond with a smile or a wave. You should also encourage every single adult, and older children too, to join in the singing of this greeting song.

Never expect all the children to join in singing all the songs. Both singing and doing actions at the same time are difficult for young children, but are much more likely if the adults are doing it too. Next move on to a couple of action rhymes. Keep the actions simple, starting with only one or two verses and building up until the children are familiar with the songs. Always try to have one well-known action rhyme and only introduce one new one in any session.

Make sure all the adults model the actions, especially if you are reading unfamiliar words or playing an accompaniment. Some of the younger or less mature children might be helped by a hand-over-hand prompt. Take the songs slowly to give the children time to respond.

Then turn to looking and listening games. Take the chance throughout all the activities to praise good looking and listening, naming the children who are succeeding and trying to name all of them at some point.

While you come back to the circle and rest from your movement, a spoken rhyme will provide a useful remission. Finally, choose activities for a 'band time'. Bring in a box of musical instruments which should have been hidden out of sight for the first part of the session.

Allow the children to choose their own instruments, allowing non-ambulant children time to crawl, bottom-shuffle or be lifted to the box in order to take part in the choosing. I always include a grand march around the room as the children play their instruments and start and stop to the music. Always finish with the same 'goodbye' song, again naming each child and encouraging a look, a smile or a wave.

How does it work?
The approach was evaluated using checklist information on the children with special needs, and questionnaire and interview information from the early years educators. All settings continued to use the approach long after training. They felt that the approach increased both their own and the children's confidence and it encouraged all the children to join in.

Many educators reflected on the positive changes they had seen in all the children's motivation, behaviour and confidence and how this was also generalising to other learning situations. Many considered that progress was linked to the children's enjoyment of the music sessions, their better ability to look and to listen in this kind of approach, their response to the familiar routine and their increased confidence.

The approach has also been shown to improve the developmental skills of children who have SEN, perhaps because it uses routines and builds confidence over time. However, early years educators have found it to be an approach for *all* children and it has therefore proved to be a practical way of delivering the early years curriculum inclusively.

Finding out more
The Music Makers Approach: inclusive activities for young children with special educational needs by Hannah Mortimer (2000) is available from NASEN at 4–5 Amber Business Village, Amber Close, Amington, Tamworth, Staffordshire B77 4RP.

CHAPTER 10:
A visionary approach is what's needed

Twinks Read

Advice for those working with the visually impaired

About 80% of all information entering the brain is received visually. Vision is a cognitive act which enables us to look at an object and not only identify it, but determine its size, movement, texture, colour, form and shape. Observing a baby, we are able to see how vision, hearing, communication, mobility, social and emotional needs all combine to form the emerging child. This means that all five senses are able to draw meaning at the same time from each event that is happening in the environment.

It is not difficult, therefore, to understand that the delay in the development of one of these skills will have a direct impact on the acquisition of others. There are many disorders of the eye, and children will not know if their eyes are functioning properly. They will accept their condition as the norm and their entire development and personality may be affected if vision is impaired.

A visual impairment can arise from a considerable number of causes from the very mild and commonplace to the more rare condition of total blindness. Most young children's eye problems are congenital (present from birth), with a small percentage developing a visual impairment after birth through injury or illness.

The majority of children diagnosed as being visually impaired do have some useful vision. This means that even though there is a problem with the eye, it is essential that this limited vision is maximised from a very early age so that the young developing child can form concepts of the world, and so develop a basis for future learning to take place.

Early identification

Early identification followed by intervention and support can not only increase the child's potential but also help the families to play an active role in their child's education. Early intervention is the key to success for visually impaired children so that both visual stimulation and training can take place as early as possible.

The carers, as well as the child, need an understanding of the effects of visual impairment and an assurance that with the correct support and advice, visual difficulties can be overcome. Although the amount of vision cannot change, children will get better at interpreting and making use of their other senses.

Today, most visually impaired children will be educated in mainstream settings, so any one of us might become involved in coping with the special educational needs and the necessary impacts of inclusion. The majority of children will have been identified through early developmental screening. Those children who present with a significant visual impairment will arrive at the setting with additional support in order for them to be able to access the curriculum.

However, while it is unlikely, it may still be possible that less significant impairments could go undiagnosed. Therefore, those working in the early years should be alert to indications of possible visual problems. Any of the following could indicate bad eyesight:

Physical signs
- unusual head posture.

- work held at unusual distance or angle.

- frowning, squinting or facial grimaces when looking at books.

- headache or dizziness during visual activities.

- covering or closing one eye.

- aversion to bright light.

- clumsy, awkward movements.

- unusual head position or 'nodding head movements'.

Learning activities
- confusing similar shaped letters, pictures or symbols.

- unexplained delay in reading.

- short attention span in visual tasks.

- using the finger as a marker continuously in reading.

- reversing letters or symbols.

- poor hand-eye coordination.

- inability to copy work from the board.

- inability to identify known objects in a crowded picture.

Play activities
- reluctance to take part in physical activities.

- clumsiness and a tendency to bump into objects.

- hovering on the edge of the playground.

- walking 'carefully'.

- poor balance and fear of heights.

Some of these problems may not relate to visual difficulties, but a screening test (conducted by a health visitor, a GP or an optometrist) could eliminate any concerns.

Adapting the environment
If you have a visually impaired child in your setting, there are implications for learning materials and classroom management.

Toys and games

These should have bright contrasting colours with a combination of movable parts, noise-making facilities, interesting textures and be of varying sizes and weights.

Reading and writing materials

Books, pictures and texts should be bold and clear with good contrast. A consideration of the optimum print size will need to be made. Contents should be well spaced with an uncluttered layout. Writing instruments should provide a dark line with good contrast, for example, soft pencil or dark nylon tip pen. Avoid shiny paper as this causes glare. At group times, children may need their own copy of the book or text. Some of the books may need enlarging, or have additional tactile representations.

Other considerations

Within the environment of the classroom or nursery, it may be necessary to look at some of the following ideas in order to maximise every opportunity for the visually impaired child. Wherever possible, classroom equipment and furniture should remain in the same position, as the visually impaired child will have had to learn every aspect of the room.

Visual displays should be clear and not too cluttered, easily accessible for close examination and mounted at eye level. They should also incorporate strong colour contrast. Storage areas which are used by the children should be labelled, used consistently, easily accessible and kept tidy.

You should pay attention to the working position too. The child must be seated at an appropriate-sized chair and table so that their feet are on the floor. The child should be positioned close to the focus of any activity. An angled board may be necessary to provide a more comfortable position for reading or close work. Computers will need to be positioned to avoid glare and be at the correct height. Any specialist equipment will need to be accessible within the room.

Communication

Difficulties in observing and subsequently being able to copy mouth movements can result in poor linguistic skills. In everyday speech, we link objects with words and give names to things that we see. Sighted children are curious about what they see and so continually make comment.

Visually impaired children are unable to interpret non-verbal signals and often have difficulty making eye contact. They need first-hand experiences combined with opportunities to talk. Language needs constant reinforcement and it is essential that the child is always addressed by name in order to involve him or her in the activity. He or she will require commentary on forthcoming activities and will need consistent vocabulary with continuous reinforcement. Be consistent by using the same words.

Cognitive development

Visual impairment affects cognitive development because there are reduced opportunities for incidental learning. The relationship of objects to each other and the consequent nature of cause and effect need to be directly taught. Learning about self-image may take longer as there are fewer opportunities for observational learning.

While visually impaired children have difficulty in understanding where things are in the environment, they also experience difficulty in learning where they are themselves within their environment, which affects the development of their own self-image. The recognition of familiar faces and objects helps develop a sense of security. Sighted children learn consistency because they are able to see evidence of it around them.

Social development is also affected by lack of opportunities to be in control of situations and lack of opportunity to observe social behaviours. Allow extra time for non-visual information to be processed.

Movement
Reduced incentive for movement at birth (because of lack of visual motivation) often results in some delay in both fine and gross movements. Sighted children learn by imitation, but visually impaired children are not able to easily copy movement skills and will have to practise. Create as many opportunities as possible for independent exploration of the environment.

CHAPTER 11:
Awareness is crucial for success

Diane Blackmore

How can early years practitioners help deaf children on their learning journey?

There are two main types of deafness that affect pre-school children: conductive deafness, which is temporary and fluctuating, and sensori-neural, which is permanent. Conductive deafness is by far the most common and affects some 25% of all pre-school children.

The incidence of permanent deafness is far less. One child in 1,000 is diagnosed before the age of three with a significant hearing loss that may impact on their communication skills, in particular their language development. Most early years practitioners feel the need for specific guidance and practical help when a pupil with a significant and permanent level of hearing loss is placed with them for the first time.

Advice and support should be available from the local advisory service for deaf pupils via a peripatetic/visiting teacher of the deaf. If you are concerned about a child in your class, you should:

- Ask the parents or carers if the child has had any hearing problems in the past.

- Request that the child has a hearing test (which is usually carried out at a GP practice).

- Ask the LEA advisory teacher of the deaf if the child is known to their service.

Deafness varies widely in nature and degree. It can affect the ability to hear high frequency sound only, or the ability to hear across the frequency range. It can affect both ears (bilateral hearing loss) or only one ear (unilateral hearing loss) and it may be permanent or fluctuating, mild, moderate, severe or profound, congenital or acquired at any stage after birth.

Conductive deafness

Conductive hearing loss occurs in either the outer or middle ear. It may be, for example, glue ear, malformation of the middle ear bones or a perforated eardrum. The loss may be mild, moderate or fluctuating. Amplifying sounds and paying close attention to appropriate position and seating in a classroom can overcome many potential difficulties.

Glue ear

This is by far the most common cause of hearing loss in pre-school children. When a child has 'glue ear', the eustachian tube becomes obstructed, often by adenoids at the back of the nose and throat, so that air cannot enter the middle ear cavity.

As a result, fluid is produced in the cavity and this affects the movements of the bones in the middle ear. This may clear up without intervention, or the fluid may become thicker, until it has the consistency of glue. Treatment may involve medication or sometimes surgery.

Occasionally, conductive hearing loss is caused by congenital malformation of the ear. The National Deaf Children's Society (Tel: 020 7490 8656) has useful information sheets about fluctuating hearing loss in children.

Sensori-neural deafness

Sensori-neural deafness occurs when there is damage to the inner ear, either to the cochlea or to the auditory nerve to the brain. Conditions affecting the inner ear are permanent and often have serious implications for hearing. Genetic factors, illness or accident can cause sensori-neural deafness.

Mixed hearing loss

A mixed hearing loss involves both the middle and inner ear. Children with sensori-neural hearing loss are as prone as anyone else to temporary middle ear disorders, causing an additional conductive hearing loss. It is therefore essential that the condition is recognised and dealt with as soon as possible.

Early identification

By the age of three, most children with a significant hearing loss will have been identified. It is still absolutely vital that early years practitioners are aware of the impact of deafness for language and social development in order to offer support, and possibly identify an undetected hearing loss. All of the following are possible warning signs of an undetected hearing loss:

- The child may be noticeably inattentive for no obvious reason.

- The child may have an abnormal tendency to daydream.

- Instructions may be misunderstood and the child may say or do the wrong thing, often smiling or nodding beforehand.

- The child may ask questions about something already (recently) explained.

- The child may behave erratically.

- The child is straining to listen.

- The child pays close attention to the teacher's face.

- The child has limited vocabulary and greater than average difficulty learning new words.

- The child has difficulty locating who is speaking in large area/noisy settings.

- The child often says 'eh?' or 'what?' and often asks for repetition.

- The child displays levels of anxiety and frustration that are difficult to explain.

It is particularly important to look out for the following in young children:

- unexpectedly poor language skills and/or poor speech with some word endings missing;

- an abnormally loud or quiet voice;

- greater than average difficulty with rhymes and sounds;

- unexpectedly slow progress with learning to read;

- difficulty following or understanding a story line when the teacher reads to the class;

- frequent colds, ear infections/catarrh;

- erratic educational performance which varies from month to month.

What can I do to help?
There are many ways you can help a child with hearing problems:

- Speak clearly, at a natural rate.

- Look at the pupil when speaking to them and make sure your face is well lit. (Children with a hearing loss may need to lip-read, even though they do not appear to do this very consciously. They therefore need to see the speaker's face.)

- Keep background noise down and pay attention to the listening conditions and classroom acoustics.

- Gain the child's attention before starting or changing subject.

- Make good use of visual materials.

- Rephrase rather than repeat when a child has misheard, using new vocabulary.

- Deliberately include children in group conversations and check understanding more than you might otherwise do.

- Remember that children always nod when asked 'can you hear me?'

- React with patience and sensitivity to occasional misunderstanding.

- If necessary, take advice from a teacher of the deaf about listening games and other strategies which may help.

- Be aware that children with a hearing loss may not be able to hear all the sounds of speech. They may have difficulty acquiring phonics. For example, the following phonemes are very difficult for a child with a high frequency loss: s/t/f/sh/ch/h. Children may have difficulty with hearing word endings.

- Also be aware that processing information might take longer. A pupil with hearing problems needs more time to 'think' about what has been said.

Hearing aids
It is important to know that hearing aids do not restore hearing to normal and that they make all sounds louder. This means that background noise is a problem. So:

- Always be aware of noisy areas when talking to the child, for example, the home corner or the activity table.

- Children using hearing aids do get tired, so try to make sure that they have access to a quiet area for part of the day.

- When talking to the child you need to be close; hearing aids do not work well at a distance.

Deaf children, like hearing children, learn through experience and interaction with others. Even if the child is not talking much, it is important to continue talking with the child at the appropriate level. Try to create situations that encourage communication and conversation, rather than asking questions.

Playing in the shop or home corner, for example, is ideal as this maximises the amount of meaningful interaction between the adult and the child. Spend a short time each day, in a quiet space, on a game or activity. Make sure that you sit at the same height as the child, as this makes it easier for them to look and listen to you. Incorporate listening games and music into the child's day. Provide as many visual clues as possible.

And finally...
The impact of deafness extends beyond the physical characteristics of hearing loss. The way society, teachers and peer groups perceive deafness is crucial, because negative attitudes and stereotypes have negative effects. There is no direct correlation between deafness and intelligence. The normal range of intelligence is observed among deaf pupils and therefore we should always maintain high expectations.

* Further information on hearing impairment in young children can be found in a variety of RNID guidelines publications. Call 020 7296 8000 for details.

CHAPTER 12:
Children need to have total access

Anne Fowlie

Children with physical disabilities should be provided with access to every activity
There are still problems going out into the world outside the nursery if you have a child in a wheelchair, as many buildings do not have ramped access and lifts are not always available to upper floors. If we are going to change attitudes in the future, we need to feel confident that we can accept children with physical disabilities into all our educational settings and provide them with access to every activity.

Cerebral palsy is a disorder that affects people's motor skills, muscle tone and muscle movement. A child with cerebral palsy has difficulty coordinating and controlling his or her muscles and even the 'simple' act of remaining still can prove very difficult. Above 5% of premature infants are diagnosed with cerebral palsy and the overall incidence of the disorder in children coming into nursery education is rising, as an increasing number of these babies are surviving into childhood.

Symptoms lie along a spectrum of severity. An individual may have difficulty with fine motor tasks, such as drawing or cutting with scissors; experience trouble with maintaining balance and walking; or be affected by involuntary movements, such as uncontrollable writhing of the limbs or drooling.

However, contrary to common belief, cerebral palsy does not always cause profound disability. While a child with severe cerebral palsy might be unable to walk and need intensive, lifelong care, one with mild cerebral palsy might only be slightly awkward and need no special assistance. Many children with cerebral palsy have no associated medical disorders. However, disorders that involve the brain and impair its motor function can also cause seizures and impair an individual's ability to learn, activity and behaviour, vision and hearing.

Specialist equipment
Children with more severe motor difficulties are likely to require specialist seating and other equipment and resources. Standers, floor seats, special toilet seats, walking frames and specialist buggies are all pieces of equipment that can make access to daily activities much easier.

Nursery-aged children should not be expected to stay in one position for more than 45 to 60 minutes. They may need to stand as part of their therapy, enabling them to stretch muscles and weight bear, and they may need assistance to reposition themselves into a comfortable posture.

Often, a child is best able to access an activity in a particular position, which allows optimum use of fine motor skills. A floor sitter can enable a child to sit on the floor with the rest of the class. A tray attached to a wheelchair can place activities in a good position for a child. A specialist tricycle can aid mobility around the playground.

Working as a team
Partnership with therapists is essential in developing skills to access the curriculum for a child with physical disabilities. These may well include a physiotherapist (for gross motor skills), an occupational therapist (for fine motor skills) and a speech and language therapist.

No teacher can be expected to take on the role of a therapist, but nor can therapy goals be achieved in one session a week! In an effective partnership, teachers can feel more confident as part of a support team and are then able to include therapy programmes as part of their daily classroom activities.

Although therapy targets are specific to individual children, there are many common targets which are appropriate to a wide range of children and which can be practised throughout the day, developing those basic skills essential for all learning.

Developing basic skills
Because of their physical limitations, many children who are confined to a wheelchair have missed out on the early experiences of exploring their immediate environment.

- **Exploring an ever-widening environment:** ranging from the concerns of the room, through the other areas of the building and then outside, referring to objects both close up and as they recede into the distance again, recreates those exploratory experiences missed in the early months.

- **Isolating the index finger for fine manipulation:** the index finger is used to point accurately at small objects and for many other daily activities. Later, it will be valuable for communication aids and keyboard skills. Activities should involve poking, pushing, pulling, finger painting, often in conjunction with rhymes, songs and games.

- **Developing a pincer grasp (which involves bringing the thumb and index finger together):** it enables the fine motor activity of picking up small objects and holding a pencil, brush or spoon, for example, in a tripod grasp. Activities that develop this include those involving sorting small objects, inset puzzles, magnetic boards, turning the pages of a book, finger puppets and so on.

- **Eye/hand coordination:** this helps the eyes and body muscles to work together for a motor action such as reaching out for an object. If possible, establishment of the dominant hand is important. Activities can involve reaching in various directions, positioning objects in relation to other objects, pouring water and sand.

- **Proprioception (the position of our body in space):** it helps children to appreciate the results of particular body movements. Children with difficulty in this area will have poor body awareness which will lead to difficulties with dressing, copying, drawing and so on. Activities should include learning their own body parts and associated vocabulary.

- **Visual perception:** this is often a poorly developed skill in children with physical disabilities. It will result in a child having difficulties in recognising objects, pictures, letters and numbers, which will eventually lead to poor performance in all areas of the curriculum.

  It is important to assess a child's ability to pick out an object from a busy detailed picture. Adjustment can be made to materials by using clear, uncluttered pictures and confining the information on a page to that which is essential. Children with problems with visual perception will have great difficulty visually transferring information from a vertical surface on to a horizontal one.

- **Weight-bearing on flat hands:** children have greater independence if they are able to strengthen their arms to bear the weight of their body in crawling, kneeling and sitting. It also develops upper arm strength which aids wheelchair mobility, transference and independence. Activities that encourage pushing, pulling and lifting, and throwing beanbags of increasingly heavy weights will help develop this strength.

Practical ideas for inclusion

When activities and games are devised to aid the learning of colour, size, shape, numbers and letters, for example, it is important to devise how the activity can be played by all the children (including those with a physical disability) considering placement of items, size of objects, adaptation of cards and containers, and the introduction of specific utensils. Here are a few examples:

- Use activities involving spoons to pick up and transfer objects, help feeding and self-help skills.

- Attach cards to foam or polystyrene sheets to make them easier to grasp and pick up.

- Attach cards to wooden blocks to facilitate moving them or picking them up.

- Use adhesive velcro tape to attach objects to surfaces. It can also be used to adapt clothing and shoes to encourage independent dressing.

- Use a variety of tongs and tweezers to encourage finger dexterity.

- Use spring-loaded clothes pegs, hair clips and paper clips with a range of strengths in their springs for different pegging activities.

- Attach self-adhesive magnetic tape or metal paperclips to objects and cards so that they can be picked up by a magnet.

- Use large dice accessible to all children.

- Use pointers which can be spun round, or switch controlled, to point to numbers, letters or colours.

- Use felt-tip pens rather than pencils so that drawings can easily be seen.

- Attach keyrings to zip fasteners: they can make them much more accessible.

Working with parents

It is also important to remember that before they arrive at the nursery door, the parents of a child with physical disabilities have often already experienced an endless round of visits to doctors, consultants and paediatricians, physiotherapists, occupational therapists and speech and language therapists.

They will need support to share their emotions and anxieties and to help them plan for the future. It takes time, effort and understanding to support such vulnerable parents and they can often be feeling a see-saw of emotions from guilt through to fear. At the same time, they have a wealth of experience to bring with their child's disability which can ease the transition into the nursery and be a sound starting point for a fruitful and supportive partnership.

CHAPTER 13:
Helping pupils with problems of behaviour

Marion Bennathan

Why nurture groups could well be the solution for young children with emotional and behavioural difficulties

Present day educational policy is about inclusion, about educating children whenever possible in mainstream school. 'The one group which presents schools with special challenges', to quote the DfEE's Green Paper *Excellence for All Children: Meeting Special Educational Needs* (1997), are children with emotional and behavioural difficulties (EBD).

They may be acting out, spoiling school for the rest of their class, or miserable, withdrawn, failing to learn. They make the best of teachers feel defeated, upset and angry, cause concern for everybody's sake, their own included, and with the current drive for good attainments, may be one stress too many so that they add to the exclusion statistics.

Nurture groups, which have been around for 30 years, have a long track record of helping extremely troubled and troublesome children to settle in mainstream school and do well. They have been recommended as effective intervention in the Green Paper and in subsequent policy documents, and as a result many LEAs are now setting them up.

Case study: Darren's story

Darren is one of hundreds of children who have had their life chances enhanced by them. When Darren was in infants school, his school reported 'he cannot share and cannot play with the others without fighting. He swears, kicks, bites, refuses to cooperate and disrupts everybody's work. He seems to feel that nobody likes him and everyone is against him.

'At home, the children witness violent fights. His mother is concerned about her children but her control is punitive. If Darren misbehaves, his clothes are taken away and he is kept in all weekend. He is made to sit in the bath for an hour at a time. He has almost no toys.'

Darren was quickly placed in the school's nurture group, without which he would certainly have had to be excluded. At first, there were episodes of violent and dangerous behaviour and tantrums, often followed by periods of calm in which he did some work.

After about two months, his silly and rude behaviour began to be mixed with concern and thoughtfulness for his teacher, but trust in people was still limited and he still had wild fits when his work was praised. After one term, he was greatly improved and only had three or four tantrums in half a term.

At this time, his mother was in hospital, and after a violent tantrum because he was asked to give another child a turn on the scooter, he sobbed, put his arms round the teacher and for the first time, she felt that he believed that she cared for him.

Following this, he steadily improved in his behaviour and work and in his interest in the world around him. He took on a lot more responsibility at school and at home and two terms after admission to the group, he was helpful and polite.

After three terms, a new and very aggressive boy came into the group. Darren commented, 'I used to be a bit like that' and did not seem to like what he saw. He was put back into his ordinary class as it was feared he might be disturbed by the aggressive behaviour, and he was said to be 'marvellous'.

He remained in the infants school for one more term and transferred without difficulty to the junior school. Five terms after leaving the nurture group, he was described as charming and well-liked by his teacher who found him very helpful and cooperative, 'thoroughly nice'. He played well with the other children and had a fantastic sense of humour.

How do nurture groups work?
The rationale for nurture groups comes from the concept of parent-child attachment. Through a secure, close relationship, babies rapidly learn, intellectually, socially and emotionally. They explore their surroundings with confidence, develop a good sense of themselves and so good foundations are laid for later learning.

When children, for whatever reason, have not been given reasonable care, they lack many of the skills needed to cope with school. They will not have been taught to share, to relate to others and they may have no trust in adults. They may be afraid to venture or they may act aggressively as the only way they know of protecting themselves. They experience school as frightening and they do not settle and progress.

To quote Marjorie Boxall, founder of nurture groups: 'The child who has not experienced satisfactorily (this) early nurture-based stage of learning will not be able to engage with normal age-appropriate school provision and will fail if the loss is not quickly made good. The task of the nurture group is to give the child the opportunity to go through these missed experiences by creating a setting conducive to early developmental learning.'

Nurture groups provide this by having classes where a teacher and a learning support assistant work with ten to 12 children. The children register with their normal class, are collected by the group teacher or assistant, spend most of the day in the group room, returning to their class usually for the last session of the day.

The room has the ambience of a nurturing home, soft furniture, a cooking area where food is prepared and shared; there is story-time, play and focused adult attention. There are also explicit and regular work routines. The discipline needed to manage in a group taking turns – waiting, choosing, finishing something, putting things away – is carefully rehearsed.

The teacher and assistant work closely together, demonstrating adult cooperation, sharing, discussing – often different from the adults the children have previously known. They respond to each child at whatever emotional stage he or she may be. Growth, not pathology, is the focus.

Language is important: everything is explained and the adults ensure that each child is listening and understanding. The message to the children is that they are accepted and valued; as they begin to believe this, as their unmet early needs are allowed to be expressed, the children develop trust. They begin to feel safe, to learn, to explore, to ask questions, to make sense of their experiences and to put them into words.

This leads to growing self-esteem, greater independence and the capacity to learn. Within two to five terms, the majority will be reintegrated full-time into a mainstream class.

The Boxall Profile

A spin-off from nurture group work is a profile developed by Boxall and nurture group teachers to help them to look systematically at children's areas of strengths and weakness and to plan focused intervention.

It shows up the searching for response which can reveal itself in the sort of behaviour that drives teachers to distraction. It also shows up the child who has grown up with inadequate support and who is defended against close relationships.

It helps teachers to make sense of behaviour that has seemed senseless. As one experienced nurture group teacher said: 'Confronted with a child whose anxiety-provoking behaviour makes no sense, the profile is where you start. It gives you insights and suggests point of entry into the child's world.'

Conclusion

The central rationale of groups is quickly grasped by any empathetic teacher but there are skills and experience to be drawn on and pitfalls to be avoided if there is to be quality assurance. The whole school must understand the group's purpose and support it. Otherwise, the group becomes a 'sin-bin', stigmatising the child, further undermining both child's and parent's self-esteem. Properly established, whole schools can be transformed.

As one head teacher wrote: 'The staff as a whole became more aware of how children develop, which helped curriculum development. The class teachers, through discussion with the nurture teacher, felt supported in meeting the needs of the nurture group child. The teachers' attitudes changed from seeing the whole child as a problem to seeing his or her behaviour in terms of their developmental stage.

'When the nurture group child rejoined his or her class in the afternoon, the teacher was more likely to behave more positively towards them. Because of the beneficial experiences in the nurture group, the child would be likely to be less demanding of attention.'

The cost of nurture groups compares favourably with others forms of intervention, especially as Statements of Special Educational Need are not required, the educational psychologist's time being used instead to support the groups.

* Information about training is available from the Nurture Group Consortium.
E-mail: awcebd2@mistral.co.uk

About the contributors

Jo Armistead is an early years co-ordinator in York. She was a pre-school support teacher, working as part of a multi-agency team for 14 years.

Dr John Visser is a past president of NASEN (the National Association of Special Educational Needs). He is a senior lecturer in special education to the University of Birmingham.

Helen Emad is parent partnership coordinator in the North Yorkshire LEA parent partnership service. She is also the mother of a child with special needs.

Maggie Johnson is a specialist speech and language therapist.

AFASIC is the UK charity representing children and young adults with communication impairments.

Dorothy Smith worked with special educational needs children for 36 years. She was chair of publications sub-committee for NASEN and the author of several books on various aspects of early literacy.

Olwen el Naggar is chair of the NASEN maths working group and an independent special educational needs maths adviser.

Judith Stansfield is a SEN ICT consultant and the chair of the NASEN ICT standing committee.

Hannah Mortimer is an educational psychologist who specialises in early years.

Twinks Read is an advisory teacher for visually impaired children.

Diane Blackmore is education policy officer for the Royal National Institute for the Deaf (RNID).

Anne Fowlie is a teacher at a special school for children with physical disabilities.

Marion Bennathan was chair of the Association of Workers for Children with Emotional and Behavioural Difficulties, secretary of the Nurture Groups Consortium and member of the DfEE advisory group on emotional and behavioural difficulties.

Useful addresses

Afasic
50-52 Great Sutton Street
London EC1V 0DJ
Tel: 0207 490 9410
Website: www.afasic.org.uk

AWCEBD - Association of Workers for Children with Emotional and Behavioural Difficulties
Charlton Court
East Sutton
Maidstone ME17 3DQ
Tel: 01622 843104
Website: www.awcebd.co.uk

Early Years Educator
Mark Allen Publishing Ltd
Croxted Mews
288 Croxted Road
London SE24 9BY
Tel: 020 8671 7521
Website: www.earlyyearseducator.co.uk

NASEN - The National Association for Special Educational Needs
NASEN House
4/5 Amber Business Village
Amber Close
Amington
Tamworth B77 4RP
Tel: 01827 311500
Website: www.nasen.org.uk

Parent Partnership Services - for information about your nearest service, check your local telephone directory or contact your Local Education Authority.

Royal National Institute for the Blind
Customer Services
PO Box 173
Peterborough PE2 6WS
Tel: 0845 702 3153
Email: CServices@rnib.org.uk
Website: www.rnib.org.uk

Royal National Institute for the Deaf
19-23 Featherstone Street
London EC1Y 8SL
Tel: 0808 808 0123 (freephone)
Email: informationline@rnid.org.uk
Website: rnid.org.uk